The Leaving

For Margaret—

The Leaving

NEW AND SELECTED POEMS

Sue Ellen Thompson

Sue Ellen Thompson

AUTUMN HOUSE PRESS   Pittsburgh

Autumn House Poetry Series   Michael Simms, editor

OneOnOne   Jack Myers

Snow White Horses:
Selected Poems 1972–1988   Ed Ochester

The Leaving:
New and Selected Poems   Sue Ellen Thompson

Text and cover design: Kathy Boykowycz
Cover illustration: Walter Boykowycz

Printed in the USA
ISBN: 0-9669419-2-6
Library of Congress Catalog Card Number: 00-133609

Acknowledgments

The poems in this volume have previously appeared in the following magazines:

Chiaroscuro: "Son et Lumière"
Connecticut Review: "Scanning the Obits," "Sunset at the Grand Canyon"
Croton Review: "Equinox"
Denver Quarterly: "The Compliment," "Indian Summer"
Emily Dickinson Award Anthology: "What Happened After"
Ice: New Writing on Hockey: "Watching the Stanley Cup Finals"
Laurel Review: "Babies"
Negative Capability: "The Bride's Story"
New Virginia Review: "White Bath, High Window"
North Carolina Humanities: "With My Second Husband, Thinking of My First"
Northeast: "Last Sail," "Night of the Prom," "Two Women Swimming in Maine," "Second Home"
Poet Lore: "Cold Comfort"
Red Fox Review: "Nude at the Ironing Board"
River City: "In the Waiting Room," "My Father's Knee"
Rosebud: "In the Apartments of the Divorced Men"
Spoon River Poetry Review: "The Naming," "At Sixteen," "The Visit"
Tar River Poetry: "The Stranger"
The Connecticut Review: "Married," "Scanning the Obits," "Sunset at the Grand Canyon," "The Abbotsleigh Church of England School for Girls"
The Connecticut Writer: "The Newlyweds"
The Dominion Review: "Compass"
The Georgia Review: "How to Tell a True Love Story"
The Louisville Review: "The Landlord"
The New Review: "Terms of Endearment," "Remembering My Parents' Sex Life"
The Sow's Ear: "Perfect," "What I Wanted," "Electric Guitar," "The Day She Leaves"

"Connecticut in March" was recorded for *Northeast* magazine's "Dial-A-Poem" service in July 1995. It was also set to music by Marilyn Ziffrin and performed by the North Country Chamber

Players in Franconia, NH on July 5, 1998. Along with "Compass," it appeared in *The New England Anthology of Poetry* (University Press of New England, 2000).

"Decorating the Tree" appeared in the anthology *Standing on the Ceiling* (Foxfold Press, 1999).

"What Happened After" appeared in *Touchstones: American Poets on One of Their Own Poems* (University Press of New England, 1997).

"Living at The Frost Place," "Echo Rock Farm," Fin de Siècle," "The Empty Room," "Parted," "The Leaving," "After the Accident," and "The Mother's Dream" appeared in the anthology *The Breath of Parted Lips: Voices from The Robert Frost Place*, Volume I (CavanKerry Press, 2000.)

"The Knowing" appeared in the anthology *Essential Love* (Poetworks, 2000)

"Springer's Point" appeared in *Heartbeat of New England: An Anthology of Contemporary Nature Poetry* (Tiger Moon, 2000)

The author is especially grateful to Sydney Lea, Donald Sheehan, and The Frost Place for the summer during which many of these poems were written.

Thanks, also, to Rennie McQuilkin, Dan Doyle, and Sam Hazo, whose friendship and support have made a real difference.

To live in this world

you must be able
to do three things:
to love what is mortal;
to hold it

against your bones knowing
your own life depends on it;
and, when the time comes to let it go,
to let it go.

Mary Oliver, *"In Blackwater Woods"*

✶ for Thomasin

☞ Contents

from *This Body of Silk* (1986)

from *The Wedding Boat* (1995)

The Leaving

1995–1999

◜ The Naming

Home from the hospital, I laid her in the bassinet
and thought of the great disservice I'd done her,
bringing her into this world with a name I could not
say. It seemed false, as if it still belonged
to the novel from which I had taken it,
as if she herself were a fiction. I carried her
with me for days, her head dense and fragrant
against my chest. She
was a pronoun that filled every space
in the conversation, a weight
in the bed, a sound that bewildered the cat,
whom I found with his paws
up against the upholstered railing,
staring over the edge.
                              For one whole day
she cried, her small face reddened and creased,
the clenched purple fruit of her hands and feet
punched at the flannel in which I had tried to confine her.
By late afternoon I was weeping myself, bereft
by my ignorance, my clumsy attempts to console her,
unable to do anything but stand there and watch.
Then I laid my huge hand, fingers spread,
on her torso and made a loose cage
in which her body washed back and forth. Her limbs
went soft, her wailing ceased, her dark eyes widened
and shone. In utter silence she stared at me, her gaze
a fact into which I sank like a body relenting in water.
Her flimsy chest rose and settled beneath
my palm and in relief and gratitude I
said it, I called her by name and knew that I had a daughter.

☞ *The Leaving*

I lie on the bathroom floor, my bed
two damp towels and weep
for my daughter, her first trip away
from me over dark water,
the suitcase with its soft limbs
of denim and corduroy adrift
in the plane's loose belly. I weep
for the islands she'll cross in her sleep,
for the fishing boats scattered like rice-grains.
I weep for the city of London, its domes
and spires obscured now by slabs of glass,
no longer the city of my marriage,
my daughter already a curled fist of fern in my belly
as I climbed the steps to the registry,
where Queen Victoria brooded
in dun-colored marble. From the kitchen window
of my flat in Greenwich I could see
the tangled chain of students from the local school
for the retarded meander down the street
behind their teacher and I vowed,
Just send me one who's perfect and I'll never
show her any less than love.
                                    Yesterday
she flung an angry arm at me as I was showing her
the proper way to roll and pack her clothing.
All you care about is order, she accused me,
the vast and cluttered canvas of her room
its own rebuke. Then she slammed
her bedroom door so hard
bits of caulk sprung
from the molding. When she left today,

I was out pulling weeds, my thumbnail pushed deep
in the earth's soft flesh, my face sprayed with dirt,
the strength of my back locked against
each root-hair's fierce foothold. She stood
in the drive, her luggage like huge stones
on either side. Now she's off to where
my life with her began and I weep
for what she'll find there, the wanting and the
getting, the having and the turning it away.

☞ The Abbotsleigh Church of England School for Girls

High brick walls, the iron gates
through which a sea of dark green blazers surged
each morning past the prefects' level gaze,
the colonnade that channeled them to classes bathed

in white Australian sun:
it was my fortress, my playing field, my home—
so far from the home I'd left I barely dreamed
another home existed, caught up in my narrow bed beneath

a purse of netting. In July we held our skirts
above the old bronze heater's gas-fired grin,
in December ate lunch straddling the sill
of Modern History, one leg dancing off the sun-warmed brick.

The glance of yellow tunics off the cricket field.
A dozen pair of lisle stockings weeping off the rail
outside Macquarie House. The day we swapped
our green felt hats for summer's panama.

The hours squandered in the eucalyptus glen
below the tennis courts, eavesdropping
on the ball's erratic *thwock* against the terracotta
clay, the *Bloody* this and *Bloody* that. From memory's skein,

still dark with tangles, I can tease a single
strand that holds and strengthens: stations
on the North Shore Line: Killara, Pymble—
where the Pymble Ladies' College girls would congregate

in shy clumps—Turramurra, Warrawee, Waitara,
then Wahroonga. Penny Figgis. Dimity,
head prefect. Philippa, called Pip, McLaren.
Helen Nettleship. Fiona Tindall. Mrs. Fischer,

sixth form French, who kept a hankie stuffed
in her ancient cleavage. Their faces
rise as if through water rucked
by wind: featureless at first,

then rinsing clear. Here comes the long
walk up the jacaranda-saturated drive
at midnight, New Year's, hands entwined.
Insisting that "we must be strong,"

the only man I'd dared to love
in all that golden hemisphere
withdrew into the night's moist palm. There
I stood in my bell-shaped gown, white glove

raised in a gesture of beseeching
and farewell—like the scrap of light caught high
in the branches of an aging maple
here in the land of frost-bruised apples, rattled leaves.

☞ *The Piano*

What I abandoned sits
at one end of the livingroom,
lid shut, bristling

with family photographs.
Evenings, while the baby slept,
I'd practice my Debussy,

hands relaxing in the heat
from the curvaceous brass piano lamp,
"The flaxen-Haired Girl"

curling up like smoke blown through
an open window. Mornings
it was brisk Clementi,

nursing, one hand traveling
while the other cupped
the softness of her diaper.

Just before she learned to walk,
she'd carom off the fluted legs
in her plastic chair-on-wheels

bringing both her hands down flat
on my arpeggio.
She'd screech delightedly and slam

the keys again, amazed
that she could make
the sound of something breaking.

One night I sat down to play
because I hadn't finished anything
in weeks. Across the street,

her window open to the traffic
and the crisp fall air, the single
woman who had just moved in

was practicing Dvořák. What made me think
that I could have an hour like hers—
a single lamp, a snarl of notes

whose tails she'd patiently untangle
before bedding down
with her career and modern furniture?

My daughter staggered in, her face
alight with her accomplishment,
and hauled herself to safety

by hanging on my wrists.
My song slipped sideways,
she began her strong,

exultant smashing. Whatever
I had dreamed I might
become, I was a mother

in her early thirties, hair lank
and in need of cutting. Tucking
two small hands up underneath

one of my own, I closed
the lid. I swept the music
from the music stand and hid

it in the bench. I turned
my back on the piano and
I haven't played it since.

☞ *Babies*

I can no longer bear
their thrumming fontanels, the bluish gauze
of skin that's stretched across their foreheads
or the clotted milkweed of their hair.

I'm troubled by their nearly spherical feet
and hands that look like something struggling
to escape its shell. The way their mouths
keep pursing at the air. An infant's bleat

when hungry, tired, wet, or bored
is like a bread knife on the air's stale crust:
assiduous, tormenting.
When I see a mother whose geography has shifted toward

the hip on which she's perched her child,
the rest of her body utterly askew, the ache
is one I've learned to recognize as worthy
and unworthy, not unlike a mild

form of grief. I feel it, too,
upon waking, the knowledge that I'm no longer
the fixed point in anyone's constellation.
They were over long before I knew

that they were good days, the last
of my young womanhood. Home
from school, she trawls her leaden backpack
zipper down across the floor: Typecast

at fifteen, wearing a baseball hat
that tries to say it all with "69"
stitched brazenly in red, she grabs
a bagel and a liter of seltzer, hits the thermostat,

vaults the stairs and slams her bedroom door.
An hour slips by: sepulchral stutter
of a bass guitar, her size 10 Airwalks keeping time
over my head, then dinner—a desultory chore

she manages with sullen, monosyllabic grace.
I used to draw her through the house
with strings hitched to an open diaper box:
Such were the commonplace

pleasures of the beast. What complex
vehicle conveys us now? Driving home,
I glance sidelong at her slumped and silent form,
waiting for that single-minded act to manifest

itself in her. Instead, she folds
her arms into a kind of self-embrace
and dozes. Thinking of babies, I turn toward
the autumn light, all burning bush and marigold.

☞ *At Sixteen*

Like a diver who knows it will take a long time
to reach the bottom, she is weighting
herself for the journey, puts on the leather belt
hung with rings the size of giant wedding bands,
the heavy silver umbilicus that sways between waist
and wallet. Around her neck a daisy chain
of safety pins and pop-tops, a penny pendant
with the background to Lincoln's head cut away.
Her ear-rims are pierced at half-inch intervals
with delicate silver hoops, as if she will need
even their slight freight to get where she is going.

Each tooth has its own little hem-weight,
their fluted edges are laced together with wire
and while she sleeps, their sharp white points
grow yellow and broad for mangling.
But she pushes the rib with its parcel of pink
off to the plate's flowered margin, ignores
the felled stalks of broccoli all lined up and lying down
like the trees on Mt. St. Helens. She doesn't need food
or any of the things it has been my life's work

to provide. At Sunday dinner she writhes
in her chair, tilting it backward, exposing
her throat to the chandelier. On her wrists,
the heavy links of my hopes for her;
a cat collar studded with rhinestones, bright
as the least of my fears. She doesn't know
that she's taking me with her. Like the two
black shirts she wears: One stays inside
the other even as they are laundered.

☞ The Visit

I gave her some change, everything
I could dredge from the bottom of my purse,
to buy a cold drink at the college snack bar
the day of the open house for prospective
students. She took the coins without
touching my palm and disappeared
down the long corridor, her loose pants
scooping the dust from the floor,
her sneakers scuffed almost bald
of their suede, and I thought *This is how
she will leave me a year from now—*
my money loose in her fist, my breasts
on her father's body, my tears locked
in her father's eyes. When she returned,
she slammed the money down on the table
before me and said, *What the hell can I get
for sixty-five cents?*

                      She walked off
in the direction of the car, turning
her baseball cap backwards, the way
she did as a child bent over a coloring book,
not wanting so much as a shadow to fall
between her and her intent. I should have done
what my mother did, I should have rubbed soap
into the carpet of her tongue, but I didn't.
In silence I drove her all the way down
the New York Thruway, the Mass Pike,
91 South—her head flung back
on its hinges, her mouth ajar, sleeping
the way an infant sleeps when the evening's
last feeding is over—so furious
and blessed was I to have her in my sight.

Decorating the Tree

She who has never known fear, a father
who drinks or a mother who throws
a few things in her bag and is gone
for a week; she who has lived
in this house for all of her seventeen years,
whose room has been home to a stuffed penguin,
a wombat, a bright red macaw, and a moose
in a hooded fleece jacket with holes
that allow his velvety horns to grow
unimpeded; she whose every cry
in the night has been answered

walks into the room where a six-foot spruce
stands crowned and beaded with light and announces
she will not partake of this holiday,
the endless meals around the long
spoonfoot table, the lace cloth
and clustered candles, the wreath
on the window casting its circular shadow
each time a car climbs the hill. After
this year, she reminds me, she may
not come home for Christmas at all.

From the box filled with ornaments, she selects
the broken-off head of a statue of Mary
she found in a junkpile. Impaling it
on the tree's topmost branch, she makes
the lights tremble. Then she is gone.
From its nest of tissue, I unwrap
a small wooden airplane preserved
from my childhood. Fuselage balanced
between two fingers, I send it aloft
on the tailwind of her leaving—out
toward the street, the sea, and the future,
trailing its white plume of grief.

☞ The Scholar's Life

in memoriam F.A.W., 1949-1977

At twenty-one I carried the *Inferno* lightly
at my hip, its bright red cover pressed
against my skirt as I walked back
from the English building to my room
in Forest East. My boyfriend, head
bowed over a guitar, was waiting for me—
skin the color of my parents' walnut dining table,
black hair, densely coiled. All

I knew about was heaven; all I wanted
was his long, dark body in my narrow
dormitory bed at midnight, there
when I arose and dressed for classes,
there when I returned. The journey down
lay still ahead of us, the age
in which we lived with its descending rooms
of lust, waste, anger, and hypocrisy
ending in the treachery of a snowstorm,
his car a web from which one arm,
extended, filled its palm with white.

At graduation I sat mute between my parents
in the moist gymnasium, their lined and worried faces bland
with pride. Gowned in black, I stood
when I was told to stand, I sat, ears tuned
to the steaming street outside the field house,
where I heard his '67 Mustang keen
as he downshifted, saw the cordage of his arm,
his almost slender wrist and lissome fingers
tighten as his hand closed on the gearknob,

tasted something scorched and salty—like the afternoon
he watched me from his place among the shadows
oil and tan myself at the forbidden quarry,
his eyes so flagrant on my skin it blazed
and shone and darkened at the border
of that jade-filled pit in which a dozen cars
lay quenched and rusted in the milky light.

☞ *In the Waiting Room*

My daughter's slumped in a chair as far away from me
as she can get, her knitted cap pulled low,
her English textbook splayed across her knees.
I'm reading *People* magazine: Princess Di,
now five months in her island grave,
still wears her princes' arms draped casually
about her neck. The nurse appears
and takes my daughter from me without asking.

Sound of metal curtain-rings
against a metal bar. The paper gown
inadequate, vinyl warming to the temperature
of flesh. The doctor sat across from me
and held me in his gaze: *You're sleeping
with your boyfriend?* I said Yes,
and held the pills he gave me pressed
between us in my shirt the whole long ride
by motorcycle home. Six years later, that same
road would show my lover to his death.

I never told my daughter he had skin
so dark it turned a dusty blue in summer,
that he played guitar, a voice like velvet
coming off the bolt, or that the turned expanse
from hip to knee gleamed
like oiled stone when he stepped from the shower.
He led me out of shyness by the wrist,
the chin, the hollow; he taught me
how to wait, contained, for rage to pass.
He wound my hair around his fist
the day he said that we would marry,
but no gesture was a match for what we faced.

My daughter counts the ceiling tiles,
the slats in the venetian blinds, not wanting
to be in the second period English class
already under way, not wanting
to go home, nor to be here
beneath the doctor's gloved, insistent hand;
not wanting to be like her mother, always
reading, always searching for a grief beyond
the little griefs by which she lives.

☞ The Asking

For my birthday this year, knowing
that she has no money to spend, I ask
my daughter to come to me unadorned: No
silver hoops laced in the curl of her ear,
no bicycle chain bracelet, no black
cuff studded with half-spheres of steel,
no rosary dangling a bronze Star of David.
I want the silver ball-chain, the tubular
neoprene choker, the thin black cord
with the day-glo chicken, the wasp
imbedded in lucite, the Maori good-luck symbol
carved from synthetic whalebone,
the peace sign, the yin-yang medallion,
the soda can pop-tops strung up
like so many scalps—I want them all
gone. I want her to come to me
in a blouse with an open collar,
wearing only the chicken-pox scar that was raised
like a pearl at the base of her throat
in second grade. The first time

I was alone with her, I lay her
on the hospital bed and unwrapped
her, layer upon layer of cotton flannel,
cotton knit, the small, sodden diaper—
and there she was, her skin slightly
mottled, a promise of hair, her folded-up
legs deeply creased and on
her wrist a bracelet of white plastic beads,
a single letter in black on each and her name
trailing off in a tail of floss that she waved
and flailed like a leash.

☞ *The Mother's Dream*

Rushed all morning, I leave the house
without buttoning my coat, drive into town,
am waiting at a stoplight when I see
the shadow-mother in the car behind me
twist and lean to check her sleeping infant.
Suddenly I know—more fundamentally
than I've known anything—I've left
my baby home. The dream proceeds,
an underwater dance in which each step
is languid, hampered, infuriatingly
slow. Traffic swirls like storm debris,
my car is blunt and useless as a raft.

Awakened by the shriek
of the morning's first shower—
angry mix of air and water
in the bathroom pipes—I hear
the sullen movements of my full-limbed,
full-grown daughter in her senior year.
She's overslept, she's overtired,
I know that if I try to speak to her
I'll get an angry, muffled *Mom*— her signal
for an end to conversation. So I let
myself fall backward into sleep,
and like a book whose pages separate
just where the bookmark's wedged
its narrow foot, the dream takes up
the story of my mothering, along with its
familiar consequence: I never get her back.

Electric Guitar

Black and white like new piano keys
and shaped like something a rolling pin
might do to a viola, it has a nail enamel sheen

that promises to lure our daughter back.
It's not a toy, the salesman reassures us,
his waist-length hair and eyebrow ring

as clear an indication as any we have seen
that he is hip and we are what we are:
two well-intentioned relics of the period

his burgundy bellbottoms would seem to emulate.
Three hundred bucks for the guitar,
some pics, a padded travel case, a strap

and then another hundred, give or take,
for the magic box that's guaranteed to turn
nineteenth century lath to mucilage.

We run our fingers up and down its slender
blondish neck, we test the strings for tautness
and the frets for fretfulness. To be adored

is something we would buy at any price;
still, we linger over the decision, love
and money's web so densely tangled

in our heads it almost seems
a plausible exchange.
We take it. Driving home,

anticipation gilds the very pavement:
Christmas morning's pleasure is already
ours, concealed beneath the station wagon's

carpeted false floor. Sprawled
across the corrugated landscape of her unmade bed,
the future mistress of the "reverb" button

wonders how to rid herself of two
such hopeless adults whose idea of fun
is to sit entangled in pajamas on the sofa,

straining after subtitles in some uncut
foreign classic while they share
a doll-sized glass of something clear and sticky.

She wonders, watching from her window
as they mince their way across the frozen asphalt,
faces ludicrous with joy, what makes them happy—

imagines it as something ordinary,
something given, like the little wreath
of light the sun's laid at their door.

☞ *Living at the Frost Place*

The day my daughter leaves for California,
I'm three hundred miles north
in the Franconia, New Hampshire farmhouse
where Robert Frost lived with his wife
and four young children. I don't call
to tell her to pack vitamins and sunblock,
I don't ask what airline or what flight she's on.
She's old enough to make her way
from one end of the continent to another.

I spend the morning writing
at my makeshift summer desk on the verandah,
Mount Lafayette a hazy blue reminder
of the obstacles that pierce the sky at intervals
from here to the Sierras. The Morris chair
Frost sat in when he wrote the great poems
of his middle years stands brooding
in the parlor, flanked by manuscripts
and letters in glass cases—stern reminders
that I've reached the point in life where work
must come before the fretful agitations of a parent.

I take the silkscreened print she made me
for my birthday—an abstract latticework
in red and black like synapses, or the mysteries
of blood—down from the mantel and replace it
with a photo of the poet on the peak of Lafayette
surrounded by his children: disapproving
Lesley; Marjorie, who died of complications
following childbirth; Carol, melancholy boy
who shot himself; Irma, terrified
of men, who went insane.

⌒ *The Knowing*

The night before the final exam,
I stand in her doorway, my arms filled
with laundry still taut from the line.
High school is almost over, everything
littering her room is broken or ending:
the cupped stubs of candles,
the wilted root-hairs of a cactus
spilled on the sill in a scattering of sand;
the confetti that's left when notes are torn
from their bindings speckling the carpet
like so many used-up stars.
She sits in a cross-legged slump on the floor,
her baseball cap pulled down low
and her Baudelaire propped open
with a shoe. If she needs
my help, she's not asking. When she

was in seventh grade, I bought her
Les Châteaux de France at a bookstall in Paris.
Night after night we sat propped in her bed,
one of us reading until she came
to an unfamiliar word and the other
looking it up in the old blue Larousse. By the end
of that winter we knew the word for *corbel*
and *truss, portcullis* and *finial*
and *crenelation*. Between us we had
all the knowledge we needed to live in a world
whose walls contained everything
worth desiring. I lay the clothes

in a fragrant heap at her feet. Without looking up,
she aims the remote at her stereo, clicks,
and a chorus of angry voices erupts

all around us. When I was her age,
I would study hard up until bedtime,
then close the book, knowing
there was a point beyond which the facts
could not take me. So later that evening,
when her light goes out and I turn out mine,
we enter together that time when all
we can know of each other is already
inside us, and who can conceive
of a word for what lies ahead?

⌒ The Turning

Sometimes I glimpse her slipping
from the shower and know again
that she's mine, those snowdrop
shoulders, lank hair tinted green
in the fluorescent light, hips rising
like dough beneath the damp towel.
If we collide in the narrow kitchen
she'll give me a little sideways
shove, as if we were on skates.
When she takes off her baseball cap
I see the track it has pressed
in her hair, like the path of a car
that's left the road and wandered
into a field and now
it's turning back. Sometimes
at night, after her door is shut,
she'll speak to me through our shared wall—
a scrap of story from school,
a caption from *Rolling Stone*—
and I hear it then in her voice,
the sound of something slowing and
turning, the yearning
of words for their roots.

☞ The Day She Leaves

I ride in the back seat of the station wagon
crammed with stereo equipment and bedding,
a guitar between my knees and in my lap
a stack of vintage vinyl albums
she dares not leave behind. I let her sit
in comfort in the front seat with her father,
so she can push her music in and out
of the cassette deck, so she can see
the city first. My horizon
is the stretched-out crew-neck of her t-shirt,
the snarl of chains and good-luck charms
around her neck, the crenelated skyline
of the haircut that she gave herself last night.

I help her father lug the heavy trunk that was
my trunk in college, that held my A-line skirts
and matching sweaters, up three flights of stairs
to the room that is her home now, its single bed
and window, scarred desk, chest of drawers. Then,
knowing it may be the final service I perform
for her, I make the bed, folding hospital corners
in crisp white linen service sheets,
the worn blue blanket from her bed at home,
the quilt with pastel dinosaurs I used to pull
up to her chin when she was nine. The college pillow,
slumped in its sack, holds up the stuffed raccoon
she made us rescue from the center island of the interstate.

It's clear there's nothing more that I can do
for her; an upperclassman says it's time for us
to move the car. I extend my arms in her direction
as if tendering a tray with tiers of chiming glasses.
She inclines her shoulders five or six degrees
in my direction, casts her eyes aside
and slightly downward and I go
to her—folding my arms around
her roundness, feeling her hair,
its blunt chunks streaked with gas-flame blue,
against my cheek. Through the open window wafts
a city smell of diesel fuel and wet concrete.

A light rain slowly seeped into the stone steps
of the dormitory as my parents ducked
into the station wagon's vinyl beige enclosure,
redolent of Shalimar and cigarette. I wanted them to
stop, to come to me this one last time without
my asking, so I could tear my woman's body
from the frame of their embrace,
so I could start my life without
them even as I drowned beneath the wave
of grief and gladness furling in their wake.

☞ The Empty Room

Unable to sleep, my husband gropes
for his reading glasses and book.
He tiptoes into our daughter's room—
the bed freshly made in the wake
of her leaving for college, the windows
stripped of their curtains for washing—
and draws back the dinosaur sheets,
slipping into the crescent shape
of her absence.

           I think of him there:
middle-aged, the gray with its fingers
laced deep in his beard, little half-glasses
crouched low on the ridge of his nose.
Just before dawn, I go to him,
lowering my body into his
backwards, pressing my shoulder blades
into his chest, my hips
into the hollow of his, the curve
of my calves against his hard shins,
lashing my body to his as I did
in the tumult of our twenties, when all
we longed for was an end to the storm,
when all we knew of loss was to turn
in the night and find the other one gone.

☞ Married

In chairs that trace a faint diagonal
across the floor
they sit in silence, reading.

The radiators tick and hiss,
the whisper of a magazine
runs like silk from hand to hand

and on its rack of sleep a cat
lies tightly stretched,
its white eye slit.

Dinner steaming in the kitchen,
children wintering in their rooms,
something in the air between them

weaves the scene together:
the argument
that lies there, dormant;

the desire that runs its slippered feet
along the empty corridor;
the joke so intimate

that it's conveyed by eyebrow
and the history that's written
in the way they sleep:

breast to blade and knee to hamstring,
his Achilles tendon scissored in the notch
between her toes and in his hand

her lightly pulsing wrist. This is what
the single woman longs for,
serving up her mix of banter,

wine, and lace: This sitting
in the livingroom together,
in silence and in ignorance of love.

In the Apartments of the Divorced Men

The apartments of the divorced men are small,
you can stand in the doorway
and see their whole lives as through a convex lens,

the way a fish sees all the ocean. Or
they are large, one room opening into another
until it seems the whole white winter sky

has settled on the walls. The apartments
are not what you'd expect, they are neat
as pins, and to enter them

is to endure that brief, accidental pain.
They are proud of everything, the divorced men,
proud of the clean white microwave,

the CD player with its growing audience of disks,
the futon that bears the furrow of their sleep
upon its back. They will show you

photographs of their children when they were young,
stepping from the doors of miniature cars,
pajama bottoms on backwards, or give you

a full tour of the kitchen cabinets, each of which holds
an item or two of use. And when it is time
for you to leave, they will follow you

to the top of the stairs, the door,
and stand there while you drive away,
their faces behind the wood, the glass—

looking like the faces that you've seen
in all the papers: the proud, pained soldiers torn
from their homes and sent out into the world
for a reason you must read on and on to understand.

☞ *Boats in Winter*

Denying himself the comfort of rum,
he pulls out the photograph of a young
girl, hair bleached to hickory by the sun.

She settles her sawdust weight in his palm
and drifts to the floor, a daughter come
and gone. Now the son—

rough pine of his body, the snapped-off ends
of his smile—is left to fend
for himself. The wife still stands

in the offshore breeze, hair blown back,
one hand holding the flimsy hat
to her head as she wonders what

he is signaling. A flick of the wrist
and she's gone, the way one might skip
a stone. And what he is left with

afterward who can say?
except that I saw his boat today—
untended, unhauled, the diminishing gray

light washing the hull with milk—
still struggling to describe a circle
on the harbor's tattered silk.

☞ *Connecticut in March*

Here where everything is granite—
from the steps that prop the baby
for her first spring photograph
to the stones gossiping in the cemetery
two doors down—even the green
is lined with gray, and from
the blood-red buds just breaking
will come leaves of waxy green
that raise their hands as if in protest,
showing palms of silver.

I have been to California, I have seen
the coastal evergreens, their skirts reversed,
blown seaward; I have watched the ocean
darken and fold, as if drawing out a secret
from the land. I have stood among the succulents,
sun on my back like a shawl of fire,
thinking of wet bark, leaf rot, grass as pale and matted
to the frozen ground as to a brow in fever.

I have tried to love a place
for the helpless goodness of its weather,
for the light that spends itself on everything,
confident of being overlooked.
I've traveled north to where
the sun stands watch like a man without trust,
burning all night while his young wife sleeps,
and I have walked Caribbean beaches
where the various blues amalgamate
to a lover's breath, less air than ardor.

But I am married to this late winter bog,
this grayscape, this
aluminum sky that when it rains
reveals the best and worst that can be said
of any marriage: that it endured.

⌢ *Compass*

You're a cabin in the woods slung low
with shadow, mattress on the floor,
jeweled boughs and gelid waters,
stove-ash steaming in the drift beyond the door.

In December you're the fragrance of the blizzard,
ice-slag in the parking lot in May
and summer rain that closes in
like tent-flaps. In the fall, you always say

you wish the goddamn leaves would just
come down and take the tourists with them.
Still bare-chested in November, chopping
tree trunks into chair legs, you breathe in

the bitter oaken whiff of snowbound evenings
with a certain smugness. You're the earth
and I'm the moon, one side perpetually chilled
while your great planet's oven churns

its various climates. You couldn't live
here on this island, where the ocean seeps
into the salt marsh, where the beaches shift
indolently south and westward, laced with creeks

the color of molasses—an island without edges,
sprawled and pliant. You're a mountain breaking
from the earth that holds you, igneous and adamant,
tundra-like in aspect, pale hair making

its tenacious way across a sea of scowl. You're
my wind rose, you're my water tower spotted from afar.
You're a walking definition of where North is:
Stay there and I'll find you by your star.

☞ *Springer's Point*

Today I walked south through a Gothic corridor
of yaupon and live oak, their branches
undulant and gnarled, emerging
on an unfamiliar beach—
a wild place that overlooks the channel
between Ocracoke and Portsmouth Island,
where the shallow waters of the Sound
take up their argument with the ocean,
forming shoals that turn a hip or shoulder
to the sky in sleep. The sun was low
and golden where it tangled with the forest,
and the weed lay dusk and silvery as a beard.
What was missing was your chosen
silence, your walking there with me and saying
nothing, the way you do in places
of such inhuman beauty that neither speech
nor gesture should have its way.

☞ Husband

Clothed in shades
of earth and ash, hair
the color of peat that's just
been parted by the spade

he enters the house at dusk
and turns the radio off.
In one arm, a bag
with cat food, cough

suppressant, wine, a pre-
cooked chicken and a dense
bouquet of broccoli. From her desk,
his wife can sense

a modulation in the lamplit air:
he's angry, tired, doesn't want
solicitude to mar
the surface of his own despair.

She waits, alert
to how he sets
his burden down.
Tonight she'll let

him have a smoke, alone
out on the winter porch.

☞ *Parted*

End of a long journey—Perth, Tasmania, Sydney,
Auckland, L.A.—our bodies folded and pressed
up together like books, Volumes One and
Two, all the way to New York. I followed my husband down
the long ramp, suddenly chilled by damp,
east coast air, along the conveyor
to Baggage Claim. *You stay here while I*
call the shuttle, he said, but I followed him
anyway, drawing the carry-ons close to my ankles
next to the phone booth, giving the weight of my shoulder
to where his oxford-cloth shirt warmed the glass.

Save me a seat, he said when the blue van arrived,
so I spread out my cardigan, arms flung wide,
while he herded our bags to the rear.
A foreign couple, older than we, the woman clutching
her husband's thick arm, tried to climb
in beside me. I said in my most polite English
that I was sorry, this seat was saved for my husband.
The wife looked so frightened—as if I had said,
Men to the left, women and children
go right, as if I had swept him out
of her sight with the butt of my rifle. The man

took the only seat left, up front. His wife
sat three rows behind, her eyes quick as birds
if he tilted his head or cast his shy glance
at the driver. I pressed my temporal bone into
my husband's sharp clavicle—as I had done
coming back on the ferry from Rottnest Island, swells
of the Indian Ocean so huge I feared
the ship might break at the seam
between my brow and his shoulder. We had come
this far together: I would not be parted
from him for such a small thing as shame.

⌒ What Happened After

The day it happened they found me
submerged in a quilt on the sofa watching
t.v. *Why is she all covered up
on such a warm day?* they must
have wanted to ask. Instead,
they sat in the room and watched with me, together
my husband and daughter and I watched men
playing golf, their shirts dots of citrus
when seen from above, in a tree so green
and vast it seemed they could never fall.

Why doesn't she eat? they must have said
to each other as dusk fell and they scraped
the glazed food from my plate. It is
so long ago now I cannot recall
how many hours I lay there, my eyes
perpendicular to their concern, saying
nothing, wondering when I would feel the strength
return to my bones, when I would rise
from my bed and walk, feel the grass pushing up
from the earth and the green coming back to where

it had always lived in me. For how many days
did I cling to my husband like a woman pulled
from the wreck? When he stopped to buy gas
I would brace my body against his back while he
pumped, I'd feel the fuel moving through me
and think, *You're going to live.* Everywhere
he went I went with him, the stripe of his sleeve
pinched hard in my fingers, my steps the shadow of his
and he never asked why. You won't read about me

in the papers. I'm the child who was lost
and found his way back before his parents
missed him, whose ferocious embrace
confounds them, who breaks every night
under the knowledge of where he has been.

☞ Woman at 45

Maybe some other time, she said,
something in her voice slack, freed

from the traction of desire.
Since when had she turned

a man down? But this was different:
the heart never quite bestirred itself,

the hormones swam lazily
toward it. The clothes she'd once worn

for their visual perfume lay tame
on her body. She looked "trim."

And wasn't it a relief, really—
this mild gaze at the receding black

of his car, the way its polished doors
gave back the ageratum

clustered along the drive without a hint
of their fierce blue? The light

hung on in its declining shades
of brightness, finally ebbing

to a gauze. She dozed and read without
once grieving, phone turned down

to nothing but a purr. It ends,
or it begins to. This is how.

☞ *The Riverdale Motel*

Everything about the room
was wrong: the light,
creased and gray

as the lining of a sleeve;
the windows so low
only the blown grass of a hillside

rose up to fill them;
the bed loud with its own complaint,
the jangle of sheets.

Middle-aged and worried about
his performance, he hoped
this particular room

wouldn't be their last.
Then something gave
in his lower back,

and he took in a breath
that he couldn't release.
The piston-like springs

beneath their weight,
the rake of the wind
on the battered grass,

and the sledge of light
hauled across the sky—
all of the forces laboring

to make this day something extraordinary
lapsed into stillness. And isn't this just
how we knew it would end:

one hard-working, breakable man
down on his knees
in the ordinary wreckage of time?

☞ *Fin de Siècle*

A man I've loved for years
arrives to take me out for dinner, beard

a mitten on my etched and powdered cheek.
The talk right off is all of books

and children. Then, over a brisk sorbet
and decaf, he grows shifty-eyed, the way

a child does, tells me that he's tired tonight—
this the man who telephoned at midnight,

skated the length of the interstate and made it to my bed
by dawn on more than one occasion—says,

a little sheepishly, he's thinking he might drop
me off and head for home. I intend to stop

him by whatever means I've not already been denied.
But like the bellied August sky

that keeps its grief and fury pending
over the low hills for days without sending

a bolt earthward, or drenching anyone below,
I don't. I let him let me go.

⌒ *Old Dog*

They haul her in across the frozen yard
for supper on a carpet scrap. Overweight,
gums speckled, slack, she lets herself be raised

and lowered, urged to eat and praised
for doing what she must to keep her furred flanks
heaving heavily in what is mostly sleep.

When I get old, my mother said once,
toss me in a snowbank. Now she taps
the colored capsules on her flattened palm

until the old dog lifts her nose and sends
her tongue out in a slow unfurling sideways.
At night, my father lugs her by the collar out

to the frost-rimed slope behind the shed
and bracing her hindquarters with his feet,
presses gently on her bladder. Before

the first snow fell, he dug a hole
up by the rusted harrow where the Christmas trees
are dumped, the last wild place in all

their five tamed acres. Now she rehearses
by the woodstove in a doze so deep
she doesn't hear the vacuum cleaner prowling

all around her, or the snap of her leash
against my father's thigh, or down the hall,
the teenage cousins playing their guitars,

singing how they're going to live forever
and when they die it will be for love,
by which they mean despite it.

☞ *What My Father Taught Me*

The yard he kept as clipped and tended
as a paragraph, although as kids
we never noticed the debris
he spared us. He would work his way

along the flowerbeds on hands and knees,
a table shifting, weathering in the sun.
Inside, my mother paralleled his progress,
vacuuming the stretch of floor that lay

nearest his expanse of earth, as if
there were no wall between them.
In winter he would shovel paths
that memorized the serpentine

of hidden brick, and we could read
the curves of summer crafted in the snow.
On the closet shelf, beneath piano music,
owners' manuals and warranties, a journal

dated 1944, with *Stalag Luft I, Barth*
in the imagined center of the page.
Cartoons with German captions,
a floorplan of the camp outlined

in neatly pencilled x's, memories
of *kriegie* life—the bucket baths,
the rutabagas and the day
that Wyman, reaching out

to catch a fly ball, touched
the wire by mistake and caught
a bullet in the head.
How did I miss

inheriting his love of things
American, the menus copied
in his careful hand—
the spuds and gravy, succotash,

the sticky tapioca we called "fish-eyes"
laid out in a twenty-one-meal plan
called "What I Want to Eat When I Get Home"?
Or did I get it all—the steady inching progress,

the digging for what's lost, the turning
from the wingspan of the season
to the small space where the pilot sits
and plots a single blossom's fall to earth?

⌒ *Watching the Stanley Cup Finals*

Glued to the tube like all the other fools
who hunker in darkened rooms tonight,
faces glazed with blue uncertain light,
I know nothing of the game, its labyrinth of rules

or the geometric track laid by the puck that slices
diagonally across my television screen.
Still, here I am, propped up by caffeine
and pillows while someone checks and someone ices

and the crowd chants Something Something Rangers
to the boistering of an organ. My mother, a fan
so ardent she once entered the no-man's-land
known to us as "The Rotten Apple," brazening the dangers

of Madison Square Garden, to see her boys
beat back the Devils, cannot be here
to see them slash their way through the ionosphere
of hockey history. In Pennsylvania, the only noise

in the crowded parlor of the funeral home
is the murmur grief makes when death
is not sudden but sadly overtime, and etiquette
dictates an end to the game. My phone

rings in the second period. She comes right
to the point: What's the score? A short pass
down the corridor, her neighbor's husband basks,
oblivious to the hugeness of her sacrifice,

in cleverly positioned tracklight, looking better,
everyone agrees, than he did in life.
Its two to one, the Rangers, and the wife
of the deceased—my mother's neighbor, bless her—

weeps copiously in gratitude
for the remaining population of her world
but knows it's not enough. The Canucks hurl
one into the post. My mother eschews

the buffet afterward, and giving the widow a firm
if moist embrace, she and my father hit the road.
The game is nearly over, an episode
already largely consigned to videotape, but the third

period, as she well knows, can change
everything. Leaving death behind, they drive
back toward New England, toward life,
at ninety miles an hour. I've got a champagne

bottle chilling in the freezer. I'm prepared
to celebrate or grieve, as she would,
with a passion I didn't think I could
inherit at this late date, having never shared

her lust for men with blood on their teeth
and ridgelines in their noses, men with French
Canadian names and gutterals, hair drenched
in the chill sweat of the arena, but I believe

they're more than men to her, more
than the youth and strength they wear
as lightly as a jersey. Suddenly I cannot bear
their losing. If I've scorned the sport

in the past, I embrace it now with fists
and grimaces, with eyes cast heavenward then back
to where my mother's team swirls in an abstract
fast-forward waltz and, in a moment the columnists

will be dissecting for weeks to come, wins.
Now I'm the one who weeps and cheers
as she would have, had she been here
to signify the country of my origins.

☞ *Echo Rock Farm*

The redwood table with its beach umbrella, bleached to beige,
is breaking down, its crossed legs wobbly with age.

My mother reads beneath it in her loosened suit of flesh.
My father, from the sound of things, is cutting grass.

The eighteenth century cape they bought in their late fifties,
as if they knew they'd have these twenty years of living

exactly as they please, sags perceptibly earthward
just beyond the pool, blue mosaic sloping toward

the deep end's deeper shade. The mower lapses
into silence as I shift position on my raft.

From inside, a shout: my father's *Hoo!*
as he wipes his face with a folded hankie—or is it *Sue!*

as his heart makes a fist? I lock eyes
with my mother. The fitted sheet of haze across the sky

quivers, as if suddenly snapped taut. A few strokes
and I've pulled my body from the element that holds

it, sprinting across the bristling, just-cut grass,
traversing the screened-in porch, where sunlight lies in slats

on wicker rockers, dozing cats. Then, in as calm
a voice as I can muster: *Daddy? Pop?*

The kitchen cool and gleaming cleanly, whitely, bluely:
Nothing. Bedroom with its made bed. Surely

he would have called out a second time. Or maybe not.
Forbidden fragrance of the bathroom from my childhood—*Pop?*

—a mix of cigarettes and urine while he shaved.
One room opening into another's silence, order, shade.

The singing of a whetstone: my father in his shop,
bent over the mower blade. *Is that you, Pop?*

A few hours later: packing, heading north.
My mother brings me leftovers: cold pork,

mashed potatoes, foreshortened baseball bat
of a zucchini, nectarines she claims they'll never eat.

My father's busy loading my truck
with firewood—sour, muscular oak

so dry you see its tendons. *You'll get
some chilly nights up there in August.* The windshield's wet

from where he's washed it. Then he disappears inside
while my mother watches me roll backward down the drive.

Low sun swipes its topaz brush over the scene,
repeated endlessly each time a child leaves,

at the same time performing an even more miraculous feat,
transforming—in seconds instead of years—her hair from Jackie

Kennedy sable to the roan of her sixties to an ashy
gold that has more of the time of year in it than gray.

☞ *After the Accident*

the old rose-colored Buick turns in
past the rows of slush-covered cars
with webbed windshields and wrinkled doors.
My father steps out, unfolding himself
on the ice-slick asphalt with an old bird's grace
and stands, hands at the back of his waist,
leaning against the sky. My mother,
buoyed along by her puffed blue coat,
is all scurry and search as she hurries
toward me through the glass door marked
"Service," her arms already rising
from her sides. Swept up into

the car's small warmth, I let myself
be taken to lunch, I let them order for me—
a cheeseburger in the golden arms
of mounded onion rings, a cookie the size
of my own spread palm
weighted with chocolate. I eat
and I eat, as if I'd been trapped
in that snow-choked ravine for days,
as if food were love and I could absorb it,
turning it into flesh the way
they turned their love into me.
But seeing all that is left—a thinnish woman
in her forties without a car, without
even a purse, they must think
it is not enough. So they feed me and I
eat, and all that keeps me from an infant's sleep
is who will carry me home when they are gone?

☞ My Father's Knee

Home from my daughter's graduation, late spring rain,
the family huddled on the front porch with champagne.

My father, almost eighty, in a jovial mood:
one more grandchild out of the woods.

Emerging from the kitchen with hors d'oeuvres,
my mother joins us, bending low to serve

my daughter, whose tailored dress and crimson gown
have been exchanged for baggy jeans. *Sit down,*

I tell my bustling mother, seventy-five.
But as I rise to take the plate from her and give

her my chair, my father pulls me—first
by the hand and then by the belted waist—

down to his bony knee, a place I haven't been
in decades. I feel a turbulence: extreme

awkwardness laced with pleasure at being singled out
for his attention in a way that, as a child, I was taught

not to expect—my mother always claimed,
We love all five of you the same—

and a strange unease at being this close
to a man I've always loved and never told.

He squeezes me around the midriff with an elbow
locked in either hand, which makes me feel both

ludicrous and adored. Perched astride
this narrow prominence, looking as unstirred

as I can manage, I raise my glass toward
my daughter, already slumped and bored

but happy to be drinking *something*. My father's quadriceps
are spread thin as a tablecloth beneath my hips,

their shallow bowl of flesh. If a sculptor were to cast
this pose in bronze, he wouldn't have to ask

me not to move a muscle.
And should he need a title,

he could call it, "A Woman of Two Minds"—
or better, "Daddy's Little Girl at 49."

from

 This Body of Silk

1986

☞ *Love Letters*

Three bundles, neatly bound
with threadbare ribbon and girlish care,
stacked on the hearth like kindling: limbs

of the past, pruned this morning from a closet's
dense debris and set aside for burning in the stove's
black heart. With a daughter in school

who soon will read as easily as she idles
here, freeing their unstuck stamps,
no written history is secure.

Who chose this day—the sky immune,
the windows blank with cold—to loose
their lovebound heat? She wants to know

why I feed them singly to the flames,
pausing every third or fourth to lift
a compliment from their skin-like folds.

How can I tell her there were others,
that lives were leased before her birth?
She sees in this a celebration: her mother's

face intensely lit, lips fingering
another childhood story. She sits in my lap,
folding airplanes, when the light begins

to change. Together we relinquish play
to comfort, words to fire, chant their names:
Good-bye Michael, Carl, James.

☞ Flying over Connecticut

I appreciate the risks, perched
over this winter landscape
like a woman with her period
over a white brocade chair, expecting
any moment the humiliation
of a fall. Below, the house
of a woman whose husband kissed
me once as she bent to serve
canapés in an adjoining room,
a kiss so shadowy and swift
it might have been the passing
of a plane. From this altitude

there are no wrongs, only
the square white fields
of longing, roadways pulsing
with cars, each containing
a woman intent upon
her destination, driving toward
or away from happiness. Perhaps
I needed something by which to mark
an undistinguished evening, or the start
of a life of recklessness. It was
as if the whole of longing
had been quick-frozen to a moment
in Connecticut, as much a landmark
as the sudden flash of sunlight
off a skating pond. He may be

the diamond on the back of that black
snake of a road, or dreaming
his way into a thicket of despair.
But I tell you now, for weeks

I held that kiss like the fixed
pattern of frost on a window, surprised
by its delicate two-dimensionality,
always looking through, beyond.

The Compliment

He came on like a week
in the Bahamas: hot, predictable,
and not to be trusted. He said
he'd photographed the fighting in Iran
and snapped my face in all
its postures of defense. He leaned
across the table to pay
for drinks, safari shirt unsullied
by the evening's powerful humidity.
Then he winked
and told me I looked tasty
in that sweater. His stylized advances
were amusing, and god knows
I wanted the attention, his eyes
on my cleavage like a bunker
in a desert war. He said
he wanted me for one half hour
against a wall, no strings,
and like the sea my body
swelled, my clothes
receded. Then friends appeared,
and to this day I wince
when I'm reminded of that precipice
of longing. But then he called me
"tasty"—a compliment
I've savored ever since.

☞ Nude at the Ironing Board

Here the body's longings are pressed
into service as guardians of the rolled
hem, the felled seam. Here
it is possible to see all longing
as flat, endless, its features
rippled or creased but never
raised, never for long. There is a
rhythm here that holds back
as much as it gives, and steam that rises,
spent, from the exhausted folds.
My mother ironed sheets, as if to smooth
the unevenness of desire
from her thoughts, would often press
thirty or forty shirts at a sitting.
They'd hang like tired children
from the doorknobs, waiting to be sent
to their rooms. If you were to paint me here,
you would hang my clothes
from the door, use the muslin sky
pressed to the window for backlight, call
the steam "mist" and let it rise
from my ankles, lift the hem of hair
from my face where it hangs like a curtain,
holding back the light.

⌒ Falling Awake

Swimming somewhere near
sleep but not in
it, as restless
as the wind that lifts
itself, greasy and pale,
from the shallow bed
of the Gulf at dawn,
I see a man leaning over
a woman bending to lift
a banded tulip from the shallow waters
off Sanibel—his shoulders
shading her shoulders from the prickly
sun of late April, their elbows
discussing the shell's muscled turns
in its shades of flesh. Their bodies cup
the sea, faces merged in wonder
at its single, perfect fruit.

How simple their shape
against the green, against
a sky white at noon
with the steady light
of an egg. How simple
to love one man for forty
years, feet rooted in the same
swift tide that carries
them now before me
as I struggle for sleep
on a night abandoned by all
the wrong men, loose
in the skin they have tried
to take from me, bruised

by the light of this
slow dawn. How simple
it once was to fall
asleep. Or so
it seems, falling awake
to this dream of my parents
on their anniversary, bending to lift
a tulip, a shell—empty now
of all but the light
of spring and of the flesh.

☞ *Equinox*

(for my father)

I'm breaking a trail for both of us
and thinking of men who drop dead
at sixty-two with little or no
exertion. I hear your breath at my heels
and wonder if it came down to that,
would I give you mouth-to-mouth
(and whisper to your lungs,
"They taught me *that* in college!")?
Saved, I'd bear you back
on a litter made of willow switch
and vow to leave poetry behind,
study word processing. We're skiing
on the edge of Spring—a thought
that strikes me now as strangely as that
you're my father, and our skis strike
a frozen field that will be
a river before we're done.

⌒ *Moths*

There have been doors
I would not open
because of them. And nights
where sleep was broken
by their seasonal tattoo.
From my knotty-pine-walled
bedroom, circa 1962,
I saw the porchlight muffled
by the dust that sifted
from their wings. That night
I dreamed they lifted
me, Lilliputian-style,
down to Lake Champlain,
where I was forced to kneel
before the walleyed pike
who'd made me drop
my father's rod and reel.
Rooted to this choice
of death by wing or water,
I called out to the only god
I knew, and took
my chances as a daughter.

Ten years later,
we approached the light that marked
the evening's end. Inside,
I knew my father cursed
your skin, as dark
and humid as the rainy night
that suddenly closed in
upon us. On the screen,
a pale green luna
twitched but would not

move. You took my hand
inside your own to prove
that he was harmless, pressed
my finger lightly down
upon his patterned back.
I knew then I lacked
the courage to become your wife,
that if I had to choose
my death by wing or water,
I'd ask forgiveness from the only
god I knew, and take
my chances as a daughter.

☞ *A Father to His Daughter*

In my day, it was the custom
when two prep school glee clubs met
to guarantee each quavering boy a date
by tethering him to someone
his own height. The clubs would sit
beside each other in the auditorium,
and as their names were called out
mount the stage in twos to greet
the evening's fate. They called
me first, and as I stood there
like a tremolo they called
her name, and from her seat she rose
and rose an octave or more
above me. Then, to the descant
of my fellow singers' hoots began
her slow glissando to the stage.

I remember that her belt
was pink and gold, that her torso
was encased in pale pink oxford cloth
and that it stretched out
like a whole note that could be sustained
beyond the evening's end. Her hair
was pale and pleated like her skirt,
which ran up and down the register
for miles. My eyes, awkward at her
buttons, sought hers and saw there
such forgiveness for my size,
my broken tenor, the sort of evening
we would spend together,
with the colored lights so tangled
in her hair it didn't seem

to matter if my fortunes rose
or settled in the perfumed air
between us.

                I know this seems
to you a crude device for bringing
girls and boys together. But when
you're at the dance tonight, remember
that women are superior at heart
because they've studied singing,
because they know
that harmony is a gift, both
from above and from below.

Cold Comfort

(for Bird)

Friendship, or whatever ship it is that bobs
at anchor between two women on such distant shores,
lies strangely still tonight. The moon is pale
and wearing thin beyond the glass that robs
us of its waning. The lamp is on. The doors
are shut. But something in us fails

to catch the lines we toss across the room
to save a sinking need. We share
a house tonight as we did that year
in Vermont, a farmhouse strewn
with winter's casual debris. Your hair
reminds me of the dawn you stood in fear

above me, white gathering in your eyes, a crust
of white sifting from your shoulders, white
in your sleeping hair. *The heat's gone off*, you said.
I sat up stiff, and snow fell like dust
in my lap. Sitting here with you tonight,
conclusion of that fear takes shape: Instead

of being wrapped in summer's conscious flesh
we might have slept through middle age. The skin
of our thighs luffs gently as we rearrange
our legs for sleep. I see your belly stretched
about the child soon to join the men
already grown between us. We can change

none of it, nor can we summon up the snow
that slept with us that night. And yet I miss
the simple fact of life that bound us there
in dawn's cold comfort. I go
to bed thinking of what is frayed between us:
the dust that fills my lap, the snow that clings to your hair.

⤶ *Letter to Diane*

This August afternoon
of vivid lawn and swooping sky
I spend painting white
fence whiter than it has a right
to be. Each brush stroke
adds an hour to its wooden
life, each coat perhaps a year.
Somewhere in Maryland, they've strapped
you down for radiation, drawn a square
upon your chest, a great
hulk of machinery your sun
and now you're sweating with despair.
We've talked about this since
I can remember, where
it might recur, whether
you should go ahead and have
a child as if your life depended
on that ordinary show of faith.
When they cut your breast
off, it was still a loss to shape
your life around. Now

all this talk of bones—
bone tired, skin and bones—
takes absence as its art.
When they said your sternum
was a shell, I saw
a bone-white cockle where your heart
should be. If I thought
leaving this page blank
would turn the cancer back,
I'd make this line
my last. But words can only
satisfy the hours, not consume.

Diane, sometimes I'm blinded
by the whiteness here. My bikini fills
with sweat that will not fall,
even as I curl and straighten, bend
and stretch to remedy this wall
where mold has eaten through and will
again, some day when this
white yields to mottled gray, and green
moves on from emerald to verdigris,
as seen through more forgiving eyes.

☞ *Birthdays*

The radio intones the day, the hour
and hisses out the New York
weather: hazy, hot and humid,
showers almost impossible. Tearing
myself from the flesh of my dreams,
I send my legs to the floor and notice
my knees are frowning—not the first
time my body has spoken for me.

My mother telephones on the hour
of my birth. I was the easiest of her five
deliveries. She describes the dark-haired
infant, streaked with gentian violet,
and how she cried for the pink
bundle of her imaginings.

I jog twice the usual distance,
down a road whose broken face
leads me to where and what
I have been: chased by a boy
in grade school once, legs
thrashing under crinolines; the morning
of my wedding, heels hammering
down the marble hall.

In the haze cast by my pounding,
a hot air balloon moves silently
up the river. What are birthdays
but the impulse to charge each shadow
with a humid significance, brought on
by age and the lengthening light? Take
this body of silk, rising gracefully
on a puff off the river, sinking
to meet the not-yet-visible earth.

☞ September

A season ends
on a yellow verandah scraped
by leaves, swept clean
by a light rain. A season
ends, here where it began
in a play of light across
your face, this time
so quick and sharp it comes
closer to the razored light
of winter, whose deprivations
I find I welcome. A season
ends because it has to,
because the summer light
is paradoxical, golden
with possibility and bent
almost to the ground by the weight
of its blossoming. I say
our lives are ruled
by such seasons and your eyes
flash blue with the brief
anger of autumn, then
fall. A season ends
with this acknowledgment
of endings, one man bowing
to his own loss, cigarette
sifting through air while behind him
the sun turns coalish, determined
to keep what is barely day alive.

Indian Summer

The unseasonable warmth, unnatural
darkness of late afternoon on this

the first day of our return
to Eastern Standard Time

remind me of a man I met at a dinner party
who gazed at his wife—sinking

into the sofa like an August sun, all
pinks and golds, the last flash

of emerald from her throat as she glanced
our way—and said to me,

Isn't she perfect? No one knows
what to say about this weather,

or about a man who loves his wife
so much he tells a stranger,

or so little he buys her an emerald
to assuage whatever. But if this

is what precedes winter, let's
give it a name, savage

and serene, and call love
marriage out of season.

☞ The Newlyweds

That they are young, or blond
should not be held against them.
Nor should the fact
that they do not resemble
us at any age. Let's admire
the colors she wears, the swaying
greens and oceanic blues, the way
his glasses stand at the bridge
of his nose, shaping our vision.
Hear them in the upstairs shower,
singing softly to each other.
Their harmonies sift through
the floors like dust and will
not be disturbed. I stand here,

an old scar thickening
in the sunlight, thinking
of the turbulence contained
by every weather, even this
settled afternoon. What can
they know of betrayal
in the kitchen, of the fierce
love for a sick child
and the regret that pillows
our heads in sleep? They are
twins, their golden heads inclined
as they eat beneath the chandelier.
Their mouths hold a language
we will not try to remember

tonight, as we sit before
the fire warming our fears,
a telephone on the table
between us. They don't need me
to tell them how safe they are.

☞ *Son et Lumière*

Dusk descends like a tapestry, draping
the walls in armorial reds and golds.
From my perch in the backyard swing set
I hear the day's history rise
pre-recorded from a shrubbery moat:
the summoning of house pets; bath water
ringing down the pipes; a child's
protests, distant and foreign,
the noisy pageantry of meals.
Light takes aim
from an upstairs window, glances
off a banister where socks hang
in formation. More lights, a banner
of lit windows bringing shape
to the shadow of home. A passing car
illuminates the silent massing of white
clapboards, shutters heralding
a well-timed gust. Music swells
from the ground floor, where costumed figures
in robes the color of torchlight move
from room to room in slow motion
and strangely modern slippers.

Tonight I am a tourist in the country
of great white houses, resting
on this swing that, swaying,
rocks history into dreams. That I
will take any of this with me
when I fold my map tomorrow   .
at breakfast seems unlikely.

But I am taken in by this local
spectacle, how simply they live
amid such a splendor of comforts:
the *tching* of silver and glass, the small
light drawing darkness up
the stairs, the blue shawl of trees
pulled tight around the sleeping house.

from

The Wedding Boat

1995

☞ Remembering My Parents' Sex Life

They danced in the kitchen
while supper was on—

bodies pressed, Glenn Miller,
all six burners on the old Caloric

flicking their skirts of flame,
the tuneless buzz

of my father's hummed accompaniment
like an insect trapped

beneath the music—
pure interlude, six children

in ten years. A pinch,
a slap, flesh resonating

its applause,
a dip and sweep

among the tapping pot-lids,
scattered cats and chairs.

They showered late at night—
disappeared and reappeared

in full nocturnal dress.
No bleating springs,

no sharp intake of breath
and never anything

above the flannel sheets
but one head breathing sleep

into the other's nape.
I never saw my father

naked and am grateful now
for that, grateful

that I came into my knowledge
innocent and late,

that someone had to teach me
everything except the music

which I danced to,
when my time came,

as if born to it
in all that steam and clatter.

☞ *April*

When I was seventeen and tossed about
the sky above Samoa by a cruel typhoon
en route to San Francisco from a year in Sydney
at an Anglican school for girls,
I met a boy, long-limbed and heartsick
for a girl whose eyes still held the storm
above her ruffled bed in Adelaide.
He let me fall into a deep, pretended sleep
across his lap, and when with every lift
and fall into the spiral of the storm
our hearts were teased
into a momentary buoyancy, I let
his troubled hands trace palm
trees on my sleeping breasts. Sure,

we stayed in touch, and once or twice
embraced on city streets, or at the edge
of a skyscraper's sheer glass drop.
What all this has to do
with a season that ages instantly,
even as the jonquils felled
by last night's turbulence give up
their small bright sex
is anyone's guess, but mostly mine:
I flew today, just a foot or two
above the infant pink magnolia,
archipelago of phlox, and found myself
blooming again in the maelstrom above
the lawn's rough adolescence, between
two continents, alive.

☞ The Landlord

Feigning sleep in his lawnchair on the front stoop
of my first apartment, he has made it all
but impossible for me to pass. I'm twenty-two,
he's in his forties—some would call

him a devoted husband, a God-
fearing man, with his Amish beard
and eyes the color of fresh-turned sod.
Having not yet learned to fear

a man for what he might do, I speak
to him long and politely enough to get by.
The next morning I oversleep
and awake feverish, nightgown stuck to my thighs

as I stumble downstairs to put out the trash.
I hear the slow grind of a doorknob, and later
a sound at the foot of the stairs like an animal scratch.
He calls my name, and it rises like water

through the oil of my fevered half-sleep.
He says his wife has cancer, since she's been sick
she's closeted herself from him, as if to keep
her dying secret—that he'd be quick

and gentle, and tell no one. Would I just come
to the top of the stairs and let him look
at me? When I do, he exhales like some
poor crushed animal, and it takes what it took

Eve to say Yes for me to say No.
From the lace of my hem to the backlit hall,
he takes me in, slower than slow;
he drinks me down, ice and all.

⌒ *What I Wanted*

A dress, when I was young,
one of those floor-length ectomorphs that hung
in the "Better Dresses" section of J. M. Towne's,

of palest aqua crepe, scooped low
and empire-waisted, an underinflated bow
that floated like a buoy just below

where my breasts would be moored.
And later, in my twenties, a job as editor
I wanted so badly I could feel the yaw

and pitch of the office chair, which fit
my ass the way a wallet fits
a man's (an ergonomic

dream), the sunlight measuring
its bars of shade against the cream
formica desktop, coffee and the reassuring din

of phones and typewriters. I got that job,
its venal cast of characters, the squabbling
over office space and money, the S.O.B.

of a boss who sent me with my summa cum laude
master's degree in English (but a Ph.D.
in feminine compliance) to buy lingerie

for his wife's birthday, whose monstrous thighs
touched mine when he whispered, *What's your size?*
I got the dress, too, in a daze

of daughterly gratitude, but wore it only
once, and now it hangs alone
in the cedar closet, a kind of old age home

for dresses. And what does this portend
for you—my princely, my resplendent friend
in the rough black sweater and scudding wind,

slipping into foul weather gear
and stepping off the dock as if it were
a dais, sweeping out to sea in a blur

of pennants waving? Just that I'm yours,
eternal ingenue in period dress,
perpetual apprentice to imagined bliss,

bearing gifts to speed you in your race:
peach and aqua nylon, bows, stretch lace—
anything to make the old mistakes.

☞ Reading the Poem

I look at him across the room
when he's not looking: the poem

in his tight blue jeans
and shapeless sweater, I

in my single strand of pearls.
He's younger than I thought

and far more handsome: flecks
of pure green verb leap in his eyes.

I introduce myself—an erstwhile
wife and mother, on her own tonight

and looking to reclaim her lost
intelligence. We start out

slowly, the poem and I, aware
we may not spend more

than this brief evening
together. He tells the story

of his brother's drowning,
and something in the way he does

this, all the while folding paper napkins
into pale pink swans, well,

that impresses me. By evening's end
he's got his fingers in my neck-curls,

he walks me to my car
under spring's first scattering

of stars. He's telling me
how difficult it was to pull his brother

from the water, how he dropped him
in the shallows, had to press

the steaming cup of his mouth
against his brother's bluish lips.

Just as I am thinking
I could do that, he turns

and winds a fist in my hair,
bending the sure strong arc

of his body over my trembling
own. But instead of the rough kiss

I'm expecting, the kind of kiss
that women like to read about,

the poem turns and takes
the pavement with him, he

turns and leaves me falling, falling
into the place where he has been.

⌒ *White Bath, High Window*

For the cat, it's the eiderdown flung
in the corner on laundry day;
for the baby, it's all in the thumb,
while with the other nine fingers he plays

his blanket like a clarinet; and for my dead
uncle it was the plush red seat
of the concert hall, where he'd nod his head
as if to show that he found the beat

of quartet or partita entirely reasonable.
For my mother it was the ironing board
where she pressed collars double
and pondered her lot over cord-

uroy seams and the nasty box pleats
of our jumpers. If for each
of us there is a place of retreat,
a place we reflect on ourselves, where we reach

some irreducible knowledge of all that we know,
then for me it's the porcelain couch of my dreams,
the tub that I bathed in a decade ago:
deep and pacific, upholstered in steam

with a ceiling that vaulted in high gothic style;
stone walls, tile floor, and near the top
of the vault a window through which sunlight spiraled
on cold autumn mornings, and moonlight dropped

like a robe on clear evenings. It was there,
having waited all night for a man to appear
as arranged, for the scuttle of footsteps on the stair,
that I drew the last bath of my thirtieth year.

It was that futile night, submerged to the ears
in my favorite element, that I heard
my heart's muffled iambic, clear
as the pulse of a ship. And what stirred

in me then is what stirs in me now:
a love that while it may not go beyond
the love of men, somehow
contains it, the way a pond

is contained by the earth around it and seems
more significant simply for being so small
and navigable. If being a poet means
being a woman with something to fall

back on, something encompassing, something that scans,
if imperfectly, true to our imperfect selves,
then I'll show you the place where my life began:
Lincoln College at Oxford, Room 5, Stairway 12.

☞ Terms of Endearment

Sweet biscuit of my life,
I've been thinking of your smile
and how I'd steal a little bite
of it if you were here; of the delights

I've known in the alleyway between
the whitewashed storefronts of your teeth;
of how I've pressed one smithereen
after another of mille-feuille, mousseline

of late-night conversation upon your lips,
forever poised at the brink of kissdom,
their slightest sigh enough to lift
a tableskirt. Perfectest pumpkin

in the patch, your heft on mine
is what I crave, your brows so fine
I could not carve them with a steak knife.
You have the acorn eyes

of the football season, the ass
of an autumn afternoon, of boys en masse
in soccer shorts. Yours is the vast
contained candescence of a Titian under glass,

it is the gold leaf laid
by February sun, the lemonade's
pale wash in August. Should you fade,
like sun on windowsills crocheted

with shadow, then suddenly gone dark,
your face will leave its watermark
upon this page, which is already part
of love's confection, our little work of art.

☞ *How to Tell a True Love Story*

Say he pulled her face roughly to his,
the way he once grasped a coconut

on the black sand beach, pausing to take
its sweetness in first through the eyes;

or say he pulled her down like a rare book,
his face dissolving in wonder

as he fingered the leaves of her smile.
We will bring our own urgencies to the scene.

Put some obstacle in the way of their lovemaking:
have her wearing those tapered jeans

he must pick at her heels to remove;
or let their bodies impede,

his elbow snagging a silken breast,
her teeth meeting his in a kiss

that clacks like bone. Let them fail
to get it right, so there will be something unfinished

between them, something that blights
the small green fruit of their meeting

and fades into correspondence. Then let
their correspondence drop off,

a misunderstanding, a failure of passion
or nerve. But end where love

as I would have you tell it ends,
with him opening the door to the retreating light

and her falling without seeing where she is going,
or who it is that trembles there above her.

⌢ *Scanning the Obits*

What woman hasn't scudded through a stop
light, the better to observe
the driver in the car ahead, or swerved
to follow a near-stranger, the one who dropped

his lighter on the street, and finally bringing
flame and cigarette together, caught her eye
and held it, burning, for a moment? Why
shouldn't she go home singing

a little tune of what-might-be? And why
not be consumed for months to follow
by lust for details of his ordinary life?
And what if she should choose to wallow

in the wake of his indifference, to dispense
her life into the dark container of his own,
to languish unrequited, in a sense
invisible? The passionate have always known

desire's orbit to be elliptic. Why else would I,
like crows who sweep the landscape under waning
autumn's low penumbral sky,
be scanning the obituaries, feigning

nonchalance, for the death
of one whose son did this to me?
What else could her last breath
mean but the opportunity to see

each other at the funeral, where he'll
be caught in sorrow's shade, while
I am radiant in black? The gods who wield
the orrery of sex will no doubt smile

as he racks his griefstruck brain to place
me. I'll cast my kindled eye on his pale face
and, in the midst of death, I'll be the one
who makes him walk the gossamer he's spun.

☞ The Wedding Boat

Last weekend, at the wedding of a friend,
I saw a man whose face could send
my heart skittering down
the polished stair of longing:
a man I might have loved once,
had he chosen to befriend me.
Skinny dipping off the bridal barge,
night's sequined shawl reflected
in the harbor's watered silk,
I thought I saw his darkened form
weaving through the shadows
of all those thrashing limbs
like an eel through eelgrass.
Giddy with champagne,
I swam in circles, mistaking profiles
left and right until my husband
hauled me up, gasping,
and wrapped me in his jacket
on the milk-white deck. The boat

returned to shore. As slim bare legs
and shirt-tailed torsos clambered upward,
one man turned (as if on bearings,
as if on cue!)—one laser glance
of mute acknowledgment.
Later, as the party loosened
by the lawn's dark edge, his wife
(the German Shepherd-eyed biologist)
came sniffing for an introduction.
We talked of custom cabinets, private schools,
filo dough and water views,

disguising our professions in the way
that women do. I turned to leave.
She caught my arm,
where just above the sleeve's pale mouth
I felt her nails like canines pierce
the silk. Hair on fire
in the streetlight, cheeks still burnished
by the sun but downy,
like a child's, she might have had
me by the throat as she hissed
her hoarse command: *You keep
your eyes off my husband, understand?*

With My Second Husband, Thinking of My First

He knew light and how to bend it.
He could hold a glass of rum
up to the milky winter sky
and turn the kitchen autumn.

He bought me silks whose colors lay
like filtered lamplight on my skin.
I danced upon my crystal stem
until the room turned scarlet.

He drank too much, but he was young,
his face still luminous with years unspent,
with late nights tossed in twisted sheets,
with morning's ravenous argument,

his body always six months shy
of spoiling. To my Tantalus he played
the rising water, ripened peach. I can't deny
I dreamed of him long after he was gone,

I'd see him slinking down the driveway
in his profligate black car, his bike
and skis and all his treasures on a rack
while you lay bearded, patient, as unlike

him as any man could be—
or that I'm thinking of him now, your hand
upon our ripening daughter as we stand
before the ancient cider press like pilgrims

paying homage to the fall. We watch the pulp
pour down the chute until it's spread
in layers between burlap-covered frames.
The generator clears its throat and bends its head

to the task, bearing down like truth
upon the flesh of those who were betrayed,
pressing sweetness from the bruised and bitter,
pressing it right through the light of day.

⌒ Two Women Swimming in Maine

The breast stroke must have been
a woman's invention, its sweet economy
of motion, the mechanism out of sight

and nothing to disturb the water's surface calm
but the head in its diurnal bob
from sleep to wakefulness. We're swimming,

naked, in an element more solid
than liquid, of a color so distinct
from any other green I've known

I won't let myself turn back
until I've named it. With our arms,
we part and then embrace

the tide that swells the narrow cove
at dawn and leaves it, six hours later,
simmering in clam-muck.

There's the grassy point where,
eighteen years ago, I brought my college boyfriend
long before he was your husband;

where we left him shivering on the beach
to swim in those miraculous bikinis
we'd bought in Damariscotta—

stuffed in plastic tubes like wands,
transparent in the water. Now our skin
repeats this magic, vanishing

in the green opacity a foot below the surface.
If I were inclined to break
this gem-like silence,

I might confess I never loved him
the way you did. And you might say
that I'd become too much the poet,

stroking out instinctively to gain some distance.
Who would have thought that you and I,
of all our friends, would swim

the epidermis, eighteen summers trailing
in our wake? But if you're right
about me, that explains

why we can share the swimmer's cadence:
Because it's given me the words to frame
our common element, like jade illumined from below.

☞ *Perfect*

Couples, some with children, flood
the studded hillside with its grid
of spruce and fir. Some are armed

with saws to cut their trees down early—
tags have been switched by the worldly
among us, and Christmas is hardly

the time to take up trust,
with signs in all the parking lots
reminding us that we must lock

our valuables inside. As usual,
you're eager to be done with it and pull
aside the first remotely conical

shrub you find. But I've got
the saw, and simply saunter on
as if you were a tree yourself, and far

from perfect. See Jack and Jill,
who came with us, head up the hill
in silence? Last night she told

me he was seeing someone else and hasn't
touched her in six months. Isn't
it enough to break your heart (and wasn't

their marriage too perfect to be true?)?
Instead of the plump blue spruce
you hold up a spiky, goose-

necked pine. No no,
it will not do.
Why must you

be so quick to settle for less than what
could be ours? And what
does it say about the two of us

and our flawed companions on this hunt
that we seek the perfect form in nature
we can't quite manufacture

on our own by framing
a tent above our children, or by leaning
toward each other, warming

the bitter air that separates
the long-married? If earth is the base
and we're the sides, then your face

and mine together form a vertex
when we agree, be it sex
or aesthetics. Don't let me wax

geometric, it was my only C
in high school. Forget the other trees.
In your arms, I'm the perfect isosceles.

☞ *Divorce*

(for Betsey)

We walk through rooms you once loved
for the way they embraced the light—
the living room like a widow now

without its worn sofa covered in crumbs;
the music room an abandoned dream,
your son having long ago shown his preference

for sports and video games. On the piano
a photograph of the six of us,
perched in two perfect triangles above Squam Lake:

mother, father, mother, father,
child. Upstairs, we marvel at the bedroom walls,
still unfinished after fourteen years,

their insulation all you thought you needed
to keep winter out. I've brought you a picnic,
but the movers haven't finished

and our kids are having the last of their fun
in the half-filled van.
So we eat it all in the hot, bare kitchen,

drinking wine, my voice like a stream
catching on everything
but you, dry-eyed, looking ahead.

The children scatter shredded lettuce everywhere
and I bend to pick it up but you stop me,
saying you've cleaned this house for the last time,

it's Jack's problem now.
Afterward, we all go out for ice cream,
which melts quickly in the heat from the parking lot.

Your son and my daughter,
friends since nursery school,
kick a soda can back and forth

and say good-bye, wrestling a little
on the grass. We embrace the way women
hardly ever embrace, our breasts

dovetailing, and you thank me for everything,
for being your friend these past eight years,
for the supper, the wine.

I stand there like the sailor's wife,
watching you, our children's childhood, the car,
the ice cream—everything getting smaller.

☞ *Last Sail*

This is the last
sail of the season. It is clear

from the way
the clouds gather force

and force their way
across the sky,

clear from the silence
you assume at the tiller

that this is the kind of chill
that settles in and stays there

for the season.
Our daughter fills the air

with splashes, knock-
knock jokes and screams that sound

like wind
winding through the shrouds.

We ought to go
to that funeral, I say.

She was a friend,
and to find her husband

cold on the kitchen floor like that.
I find all this enough to make me want

to knock that tiller
from your hands and jibing, knock

you senseless.
But this is not the way we do things

in New England,
where the weather comes upon us

like a war
we know is wrong,

where we are accustomed
to certain seasons of hardship.

Which is why
when you say nothing, I say nothing.

◠ Sunset at the Grand Canyon

The light, I learned, was everything—
the way it hauled itself

up from the canyon floor at sunset,
leafing the palisades with gold.

It could turn the postcard
of a distant monolith to film—

leaping, almost speaking with color.
Or it could turn

on its heel, leaving its striated sheets
of landscape stacked against the rim

like flats after the play has closed.
The single cloudy day of our vacation

we argued over nothing and watched
our not-quite-teenage girl grow sullen,

hurling herself repeatedly against
the false blue light of the pool.

If there had been sun, we might have seen
the slightest swelling of a breast

beneath her pale green suit. Instead,
the sky grew dark, released some rain

and still we sat there watching
from the silence of our chairs,

while like a bird she
rose, and preened, and disappeared.

☞ Second Home

Housewives love November, before the snow
lays down its fake white fur, before the thaw

trudges in with its muddy boots.
Just beyond the ridge that blocks our view

the mountains are lined up against the sky,
each peak paler and more beckoning

with distance. Here in the yard,
the trees pitch in the early dusk,

wrapped in their thin black coats
and shivering theatrically.

I help my husband move crushed granite,
stippled pink and gray, into a drainage ditch,

thinking of coral beaches, thinking of the day
this boggy northern plot will catch the sun.

My husband, back hurting, thinks only of ice dams,
spring floods, paint cans tipped and floating

in the basement. But as the sun
splinters through clouds for one brief moment

before slipping into its mountain envelope,
and as the trees reach up with knitted fingers

to catch their day's iota of warmth,
I can't help laying my shovel aside

and exclaiming at the beauty of it all,
the lawn swept clean by weeks of wind

and washed in sudden light. My husband,
angry at everyone today, responds

this is the coldest, darkest place on earth,
he'll never understand why I wanted this house,

its useless scrawl of poplar woods,
its muddy cellar and chill, wet drafts.

For what we've put into this place
we could have had two weeks a year in Florida

for life, no yard. I lean on my shovel
and watch the light languish and fall,

I see the trees pulling back into themselves
and I forgive him, because he doesn't know

what it feels like to be shedding something,
because he doesn't know what I'll become.

◌ *The Stranger*

This handsome man, divorced, arrives in town
and all of us are mad for him, straining from behind
our steering wheels to catch a glimpse. He is there
at every summer party, silver-templed and impeccable,
talking business with our husbands, wrapped
in faint cocoons of aftershave and scotch. I've watched
him fix a woman with his cobalt stare from fifteen yards,
I've seen her try to pull away from that, to twist
her shoulders toward another conversation while her head
is still as the head of a marionette, the rest
of her body lifting and floating away. Any one of us
would leave with him tomorrow if he asked us,
if he turned his burnished face in our direction.
But he keeps us waiting, never guessing how
this fans our small desire:

                                    All those years
of waiting for the station wagon to appear
in the pool of streetlight at the corner, for it to clear
the driveway's lip, curving down to the garage, then listening
for footsteps heavy on the cellar stairs. For this
is how they enter you, beginning in the dark
where love is made and moving up through laundry,
toys, the hooks where coats are sloughed like skins.
My father always paused a few steps from the top,
afraid the door might suddenly explode on him,
his children's faces brighter than a bulb.
He'd stand there jingling his car keys in the darkness,
breathing in the concrete air, afraid
of what love might do to him.

The Mowing

You would have undone everything:
the apples gathered, bushes sculpted
into boxcars, silken grass
that let itself be cut in perfect stripes,
the cat asleep in her summerhouse
beneath the dense forsythia
as you moved closer.

But when I heard you cry out—
when you brought her to me
in your outstretched arms,
her small head lowered, dark half peeled
and crimson as a plum—

I knew the season of our innocent routine
had ended, comforts of the house
and yard, summer's gauze
stripped violently away.

That night we lay like two boats
restless at their moorings,
veils of moisture gathering
where we touched.
And while we labored, palm on palm,
to coil and stow the day's events,

suddenly I was at your back,
all tooth and claw and ravenous
to have it all: the green, the fear,
the salt, the blood, the smell
and taste of my living, breathing husband.

☞ *Reunion*

Twenty years later, you are standing with her again
on the same green bedspread of lawn,
your old dorm like a painted backdrop,
her room winking its single eye
further back, behind a scrim of lilacs.
Two kids who've never known anything
but the long walk up Chapel Hill at sunset,
which settles now like a silk scarf
on the bunched shoulders of the Adirondacks.

The same prim mouth and tilted nose,
that halo of hair gone darker but not yet gray,
she has aged the way all of us wish to age,
her smile set deeper in her face,
her skin a tawny linen lined with pink
from the California sun. A boy who's young
enough to be our child yells *Class of '70*
and like the gentle bovines we've become,
we amble to our place in the procession,
your hand lightly grazing her waist, and I,
your wife, just a few steps behind.

But I'm not your wife yet—
not when we pass the fraternity house
where I found you drunk one Saturday night;
not when you tell me you caught her in bed
with a 25-year-old freshman,
his back already scarred from Vietnam;
and not, finally, when I drag you out
in the sub-zero air and force you to walk with me,
the campus quiet as a drawn sheet,
inarticulate with snow.

This tree forms the lintel we all passed under
the day we left Vermont, and I hang back now

to let the two of you enter its shade together,
your heads bowed low in conversation.
I want to take my ring and close her hand
around it, tell her she is beautiful and will be
happy. I want the girl I was then to step back
from the porchlight, clutching her books
to her chest while the two of you
continue your motionless kiss.

For this is the way we enter the past,
giving up all we claim to have won
and letting what's lost step forward.
Someone I should recognize but don't,
his blue eyes buried in the rumpled laundry
of his face, touches my arm, says
Isn't that Kathy and Stu?
Something that is not love swells
in me like love, and all I can do is say
Yes and give you back.

Night of the Prom

It is more than the passage of years,
which in itself might lower a scrim
of sadness and loss between us
and the occasion, beginnning as it does
when the car makes an arc in the driveway,
where the adults of the family are assembled
in their cameras and old spring sweaters, watching
as she alights in a cloud of hair,
her bare brown shoulders pushed up
like new mountains from a sea of bluish lace.
It is not longing
that tilts and tinges the scene
until we cannot be sure who these fledglings may be;
or envy,
although it is true I never spent a night in May
beneath the crenellated awnings of a paper Camelot.
Perhaps it is how much they look alike,
with their reddish curls and ruffled white carnations,
hands locked like the branches of a tree
whose trunk, willowy and green, sways
invisibly between them.
They could be brother and sister,
a thought that comforts us,
conferring an innocence upon the evening air—
or two children playing dress-up
in a musty tux and old lace veil.
But no, it is this:
that when they pose for photographs
in the purplish dusk of the small back yard,
a crown of dogwood seems to light
for a moment in her hair, making these two
king and queen of a world
where to be blessed is to believe in the
choices these blossoms were sent out to make.

The Bride's Story

I'm not the mother who dabs at the stain
above her breast to stave
off tears as the bride waves
good-bye, nor am I the father whose disdain

for the boy his daughter has chosen to marry
is evident. I am not the groom
who guides her through the flume
of rice and rose-petals, who carries

her to his idling car, trailing
streamers in a foreshadowing of blood.
Her bouquet lifts into the night, then scuds
across the pavement toward an ailing

maiden aunt, wheelchair-bound,
and the crowd hangs back, chastened.
I cannot tell you what hastened
or slowed their departure, or who found

the car, wheels spinning, or what kind of fool
would mix these two occasions,
but I like to think that her evasions
were playful, that from somewhere in that cloud of tulle

she beckoned him, and would have taught
him love in the undoing
of a thousand buttons; and that misconstruing
her long look backward, he thought

he saw her resolve go slack
and swerved to avoid it. I'm not the surgeon
who unzipped her abdomen to find the burgeon
of a child in its small glazed sac,

nor am I among the wedding
guests who huddle, three days later,
at her grave. I'm not the investigator
who was last seen threading

his way through mourners to arrest the groom
for driving under the influence,
nor did I play a part in this confluence
of love and death. But I'm the one to whom

the bride has left her story:
it pulls at me like a train of lace
and wraps my nights in its fierce embrace,
a constant reminder of the transitory

joy of the wedding day, when we pretend
to choose what is already chosen
and the sweet cream of the future lies frozen
on our plates. The bride's story doesn't end

here, in the telling, any more than bed
puts an end to the tragedy of desire.
Each death ignites its own small fire,
and with this poem, I thee wed.